My First Animal Alphabet

a

Amazing Animal Books
Children's Picture Books

By Molly Davidson

Mendon Cottage Books

JD-Biz Publishing

Read More Amazing Animal Books

Purchase at Amazon.com

Download Free Books!
http://MendonCottageBooks.com

Introduction

Antarctica is on the southern most part of the Earth. The continent contains 70% of all the Earth's fresh water, but we cannot use it, since most of it is always frozen. It can reach temperatures as low as of -129°F (-89°C)! Very few animals can survive in this harsh, freezing environment.

I have included a few double bonus letters, and left out a few, there are some letters which just do not have an animal, since there are so few that live there in the first place.

Let's begin as we learn about the few animals that do live in Antarctica.

 is for Arctic Krill.

Arctic krill are a type of shrimp that swims in large swarms along the coasts of Antarctica.

They can go 200 days without eating!

Many species feed off krill in the Antarctic.

is for an Adelie Penguin. *Bonus Letter

Adelie penguins are the most common penguins seen around all of Antarctica.

They're also the smallest, weighing about 13 lbs (6 kg) and standing about 2.5 ft (75 cm) tall.

B is for a Blue Whale.

The few blue whales that are left can be seen swimming in all the Earth's oceans, including the oceans surrounding Antarctica.

It is the largest animal on Earth, weighing 180 tons (the weight of 14 school buses) and growing to 98 feet in length.

C is for a Chinstrap Penguin.

Chinstrap penguins live on rocky islands in the Antarctic.

They eat fish, crabs, krill, shrimp, and squid.

Both the mother and father help keep their eggs warm, for about a month, until they hatch.

D is for Diomedea Exulans, the scientific name for a Wandering Albatross.

The wandering albatross is a seabird that lives around the Southern Ocean.

They are one of the largest birds, with a wingspan of 8 - 11 1/2 feet.

E is for an Emperor Penguin.

The emperor penguin is the largest species of penguin; they live on the Antarctic Continent.

They recognize each other by their calls.

They can hold their breath underwater for up to 20 minutes.

F

is for a Fulmar.

The fulmar is a seabird that breeds on the coast of Antarctica.

They like to eat food that is on top of the water, like krill, but sometimes they will dive in the water for fish or squid.

G is for a Gentoo Penguin.

Gentoo penguins only weigh about 18 pounds and live on the rocky coast of Antarctica.

They are excellent swimmers, and can swim about 30 mph (48 km/h).

G is for a Giant Petrel. *Bonus Letter

They are seabirds, with a wingspan of about 6 1/2 feet (205 cm), which nest on the islands of Antarctica.

Giant petrels are scavengers; they eat dead seals and whales.

is for a Humpback Whale.

They spend their summers in the cold South Ocean around Antarctica, and migrate to warmer tropical waters in the winter.

The humpback whale is about half the size of a blue whale; measuring only about 52 ft (16 m).

I is for an Imperial Shag.

The imperial shag, also called the blue-eyed cormorant, lives on the rocky coasts of Antarctica, usually with other seabird colonies.

They lay up to 5 eggs in nests made of seaweed, grass, and mud, used as the glue.

J is for a Jellyfish.

Steve Clabuesch, NSF © <u>Wikimedia Commons</u>

A type of jellyfish, known as the Antarctic transparent jellyfish, lives in the oceans around Antarctica.

They are only about 4 cm wide, but they can have between 16 - 48 tentacles.

is for a King Penguin.

King penguins have four layers of feathers; the inner three are soft, downy feathers, these keep the penguin warm, the outer layer is oiled and waterproof, making it easy for them to glide through the water.

L is for a Leopard Seal.

Leopard seals can live up to 25 years in the icy waters and snow pack of the Antarctic.

They are the second largest seal, weighing up to 1,300 pounds (591 kg) and measuring 10 1/2 feet (3.2 m) in length.

M is for a Macaroni Penguin.

The macaroni penguin will spend most of the cold winter months in the water; it's warmer than on land, hunting for fish, krill, shell fish, and squid.

N is for a New Zealand Sea Lion.

They live on the coasts of New Zealand and some off the islands of Antarctica.

There are only about 10,000 New Zealand sea lions; they are a rare sea lion species.

O is for an Orca.

Orcas, also called killer whales, live in all the oceans of the World, including the freezing Southern Ocean.

They are the largest dolphin species, weighing 19,000 pounds (8,618 kg) and growing to 26 feet (8 m) long.

P is for a Pika.

Pikas like to live in colder climates.

They are related to rabbits and hares, even though they look more like a rodent.

They have a small round body, and no tail.

R is for a Rockhopper Penguin.

Rockhopper penguins like to jump over rocks to get to places, instead of sliding on their bellies, like other penguins.

R is for a Royal Penguin. *Bonus Letter

Royal penguins live on the rocky islands surrounding Antarctica.

They can live at sea for days while hunting.

S is for a Sea Star.

Sea stars use their hundreds of tiny tube feet to move very slowly, along the rocky ocean bottoms.

T is for Teuthida, the scientific name for Squid.

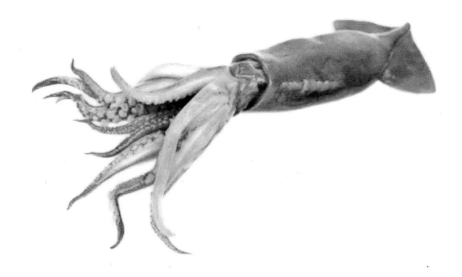

Squid can be found in all the oceans, including the frigid Southern Ocean.

Most squid have 8 arms, but some have up to 10 arms!

U is for an Urchin.

Sea urchins live in warm ocean waters close to shore, but a few species live in Antarctica.

Urchins eat ocean plants, dead fish, coral, mussels, algae, and sponges; their mouth is on the bottom, close to the ocean floor.

W is for a Weddell Seal.

The Weddell seal lives in Antarctic waters, and is related to the sea lion and walrus.

They can swim underwater for over an hour, this is also where they eat their food.

Y is for a Yellow-Billed Pintail.

Dick Daniels © Wikimedia Commons

The yellow-billed pintail live in South America and on some Antarctic islands.

They build their nests out of feathers and grass, which is hidden in tall grass close to the water.

Z is for Zooplankton.

Matt Wilson/Jay Clark © <u>Wikimedia Commons</u>

Zooplanktons are teeny tiny creatures that float on the top of the ocean water.

Zooplankton is at the very bottom of the food web and is eaten by many ocean animals.

Horses For Kids

Amazing Animal Books
For Young Readers
By John and
Annalee Davidson

Ponies For Kids

Amazing Animal Books

Rachel Smith

Ten Amazing Horses For Kids

Nature Books for Kids
JD-Biz Publishing
K. Bennett

Akhal-Teke "The Golden Horse of the desert" For Kids

Nature Books for Kids
JD-Biz Publishing
K. Bennett

Suffolk-Punch "The Gentle Giant" For Kids

Nature Books for Kids
JD-Biz Publishing
K. Bennett

Shires "The great Horse" For Kids

Nature Books for Kids
JD-Biz Publishing
K. Bennett

Colonial Spanish "Horse of the Americas" For Kids

Nature Books for Kids
JD-Biz Publishing
K. Bennett

Canadian "The Little Iron Horse" For Kids

Nature Books for Kids
JD-Biz Publishing
K. Bennett

Cleveland Bays "History and Future" Horses For Kids

Nature Books for Kids
JD-Biz Publishing
K. Bennett

Our books are available at

1. Amazon.com

2. Barnes and Noble

3. Itunes

4. Kobo

5. Smashwords

6. Google Play Books

Download Free Books!
http://MendonCottageBooks.com

Publisher

JD-Biz Corp

P O Box 374

Mendon, Utah 84325

http://www.jd-biz.com/

Made in the USA
Coppell, TX
02 October 2020